REALLY WILD ANIMALS!

Sea Babies

Sandra Markle

SCHOLASTIC INC. Cartwheel B·O·O·K·S ®

New York Toronto London Auckland Sydney
Mexico City New Delhi Hong Kong Buenos Aires

With love for Viola Jeffery

The author would like to acknowledge the assistance provided by Ken's Camera (Christchurch, New Zealand). The author would also like to thank the following for sharing their enthusiasm and expertise: Arthur DeVries, Professor, Animal Biology, University of Illinois, Urbana; Kate Thompson, Biologist, Southern Encounter Aquarium, Christchurch, New Zealand. And as always, a special thanks to Skip Jeffery for his input, help, and for sharing my life.

ISBN 0-439-33489-6

12 11 10 9 8 7 6 5 4 3 2   2 3 4 5 6 7/0

Printed in the U.S.A.
First Scholastic printing, May 2002

CONTENTS

Dive into the Ocean

Come discover babies that
are born and grow up in
the sea. Look closely and
you'll see baby frogfish
ready to hatch out of their
eggs. What does a sea baby
eat? Who takes care of it?
How does it stay safe?
You will find out all about
sea babies in this book.
So dive in!

Happy Birthday!

Some sea babies hatch from eggs. Here comes a baby swell shark out of its egg.

Other sea babies grow inside of their mothers' bodies. When this baby lemon shark is completely outside of its mother, it will swim away.

A Mother's Care

Take a close look at these octopus eggs. The arms you see belong to the mother octopus. She won't leave her babies—even to eat! Her main job is to keep hungry fish away.

See the baby octopus coming out of its egg? Next to it is a newly hatched baby octopus.

Many ocean mothers take care of their babies after they are born. When this mother sea otter dives for food, she wraps her pup in kelp. This hides her baby— and keeps it safe from hungry animals.

Super Pops

Sometimes Dad takes care of the babies! See the bumps on the belly of this male alligator pipefish? Those are eggs in a pouch. While Dad hides to keep the eggs safe, his body supplies the babies with the food they need to grow.

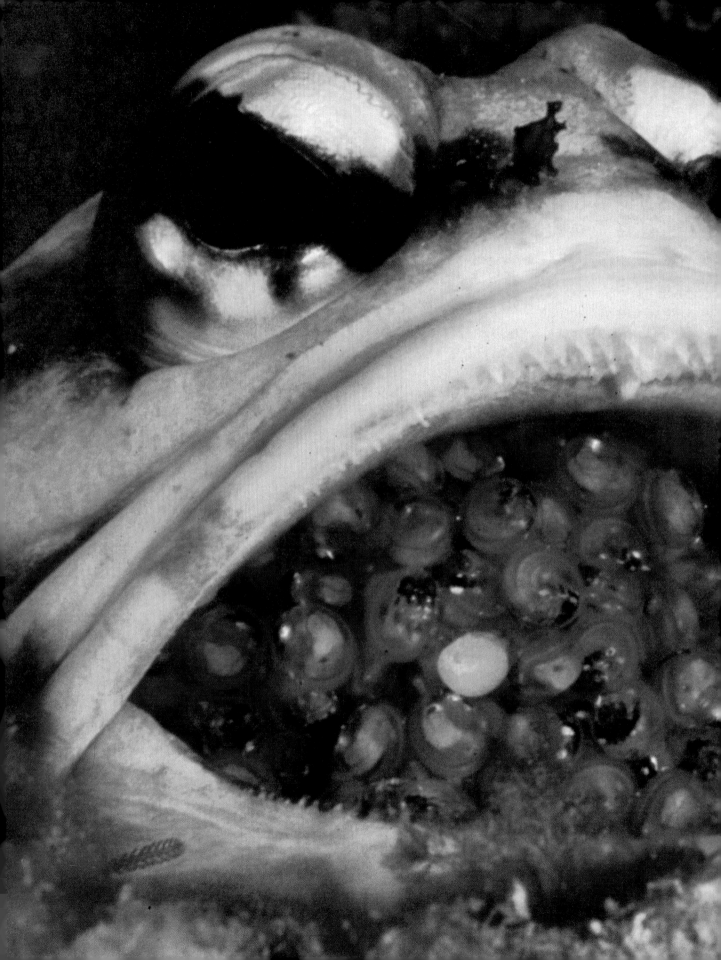

This jawfish dad keeps his eggs inside his mouth! He rests and waits for the babies to hatch and swim away.

Baby Food

Once a sea baby is born, its first job is to find food. This baby dragonfish has some food left from inside its egg. The baby uses this food until it finds its next meal.

A dolphin calf does not have to hunt. It gets its food by nursing milk from its mom.

This young blue shark has to catch its own food. Luckily, it has a mouth full of teeth! And if the young shark breaks or loses a tooth, it grows a new one. That way, it's always ready to catch a meal.

Tricky Babies

Besides eating, sea babies have to stay safe. These young striped eel catfish find safety in numbers. Being part of a big group, or school, of fish means lots of eyes to watch for enemies.

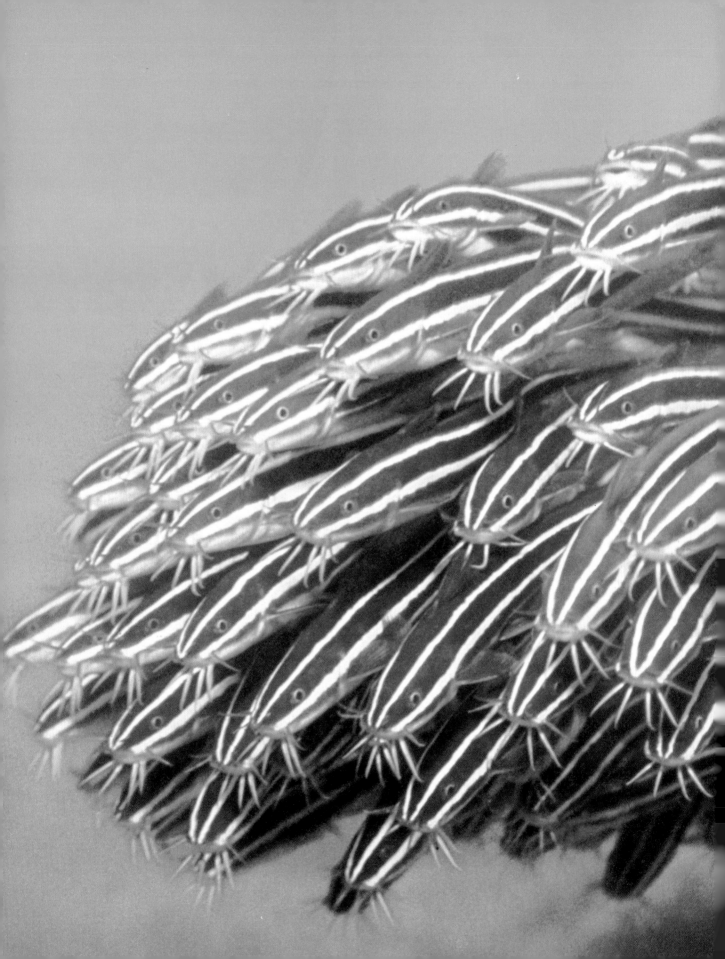

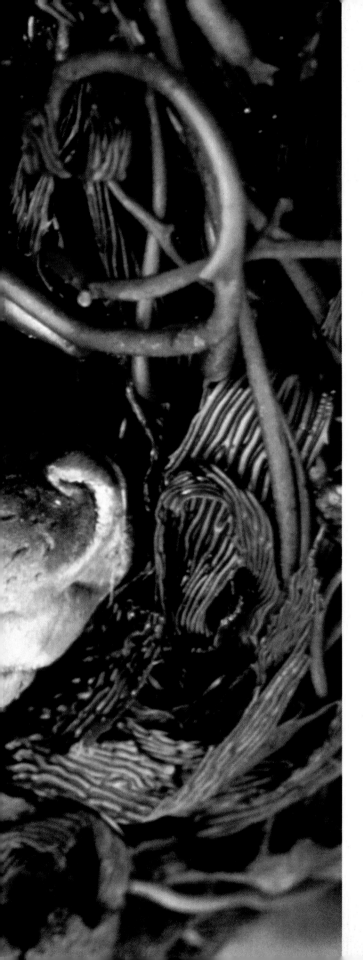

See the baby elephant seal among the kelp? It's hiding while it rests. Killer whales and sharks like to eat elephant seal pups. So this baby stays safe by staying out of sight.

This young starfish plays a neat trick to stay safe.
When a fish grabs one of the starfish's arms, it
snaps off. Surprised, the fish drops the arm and
leaves the starfish alone. Then something really
amazing happens. Over time, the young starfish
grows a new arm. And the arm grows a whole
new starfish!

Growing Up

Many sea babies have to learn to find food by themselves. But this young dugong calf has its mother for a teacher. And while her baby learns, Mom protects it from hungry crocodiles and sharks. Sometimes, when her young calf needs to rest, Mom even carries it on her back!

The elephant seal pup must keep its eyes wide open while it develops its swimming and fishing skills.

Like the other sea babies in this book, if the elephant seal pup finds food and stays safe, it will grow into an adult. Then it will be ready to have babies of its own. And the process will begin in the ocean once again.

PHOTO CREDITS

Cover Frans Lanting/Minden Photos
p. 1 John P. Hoover/Seapics.com
p. 3 Doug Perrine/Seapics.com
p. 4 Fred Bavendam/Minden Photos
p. 6 Mark Conlin/Seapics.com
p. 8 Doug Perrine/Seapics.com
p. 10 Fred Bavendam/Minden Photos
p. 11 Fred Bavendam/Minden Photos
p. 12 Frans Lanting/Minden Photos
p. 14 Fred Bavendam/Minden Photos
p. 16 A&A Ferrari/Seapics.com
p. 18 Art DeVries/Kevin Hoefling
p. 20 Doug Perrine/Seapics.com
p. 22 Richard Hermann/Seapics.com
p. 24 Doug Perrine/Seapics.com
p. 26 Tui De Roy/Minden Photos
p. 28 John P. Hoover/Seapics.com
p. 29 Doug Perrine/Seapics.com
p. 30 Bob Cranston/Seapics.com
p. 32 Doug Perrine/Seapics.com
Back cover Richard Hermann/Seapics.com